CPM ADVERTISING 101

Everything you need to know

with

Real-world Examples

Boyd Jackson

Table of Contents

Chapter One

Introduction to CPM Advertising

The advertising industry has changed dramatically in the current digital era, giving rise to creative methods and tactics for successfully interacting with target consumers. Cost Per Mille (CPM) advertising is one such strategy that enables companies to promote their goods or services to a large online user base. Due to its low cost and capacity to significantly increase brand visibility, CPM has grown to be a crucial component of digital marketing.

For marketers and advertisers wishing to take advantage of this potent advertising technique, this book will act as a complete reference to CPM advertising. Understanding the basics of CPM is essential to reaching your marketing objectives, regardless of whether you're an experienced marketer or a beginner looking for new ways to improve your online presence.

We will go into the fundamentals of CPM advertising, outlining its operation, many campaign kinds, and advantages over alternative advertising models. We'll also look at the difficulties in optimizing CPM campaigns and offer helpful advice on how to deal with them.

You must understand the essential components needed for achievement if you want your CPM campaigns to be as effective as possible. We'll talk about issues including establishing campaign goals, picking the best ad styles and locations, and allocating a reasonable budget. With this information at hand, you'll be able to make wise choices and design campaigns that produce the best outcomes.

For a campaign to be successful, picking the correct CPM advertising platform is essential. We'll provide you an overview of well-known ad networks and platforms, assisting you in selecting choices that fit your target market and financial constraints. Additionally, we'll provide you with crucial campaign optimization tools so you can keep enhancing and adjusting your strategies.

Understanding key performance indicators (KPIs) and knowing how to correctly analyze campaign metrics are crucial for gauging the success of your CPM advertising campaign. We'll go into great detail on these metrics so you can track success and make data-driven choices to increase the return on investment (ROI) of your campaign.

In this book, we'll present case studies and examples of effective CPM campaigns to highlight the methods and techniques used to get great results. You'll gain knowledge about the actual use of CPM advertising and how you may modify these methods to meet your particular needs by taking inspiration from these real-life success stories.

We'll talk about new developments and trends in CPM marketing as we look to the future. You may use changes in consumer behavior and technological improvements to produce even more effective ads by remaining one step ahead of the curve.

Prepare to start your CPM advertising adventure. By the time you finish reading this booklet, you'll be equipped with the information and resources you need to create effective CPM campaigns that will help you achieve your marketing goals. Let's start now!

1. Awareness of Advertising Models

conventional methods of advertising

Pricing and performance metrics for online ads are decided using advertising models as a framework. Understanding various popular advertising models used in digital marketing is essential before diving into CPM advertising.

• Cost Per Click (CPC): With CPC marketing, marketers are charged for each click that results in a sale. Search engine advertising, display advertising, and social media advertising all frequently employ this paradigm. CPC advertising's primary goal is to increase visitors to a website or landing page.

Cost Per Acquisition (CPA) advertising places more of an emphasis on conversions than on clicks. Advertisers only receive payment when a user takes a particular action, such making a purchase or subscribing to a newsletter. Due to its ability to enable marketers to carefully monitor and optimize their return on investment (ROI), this approach is very well-liked in the affiliate marketing and e-commerce sectors.

2. CPM Advertising Overview:

The meaning and purpose of CPM advertising

Cost per thousand impressions (CPM) advertising enables marketers to pay for ad placement according to the number of impressions (views) their ad receives. Advertisers pay a flat fee for per thousand impressions rather than for clicks or conversions.

Compared to other models

CPM advertising, as opposed to CPC and CPA, prioritizes brand exposure and visibility above quick actions or conversions. For brand recognition initiatives or to reach a large audience, CPM advertising are frequently employed. Display advertising, video advertising, and programmatic advertising all frequently use this approach.

Identifying "mille"

The Latin word "mille" in CPM means "thousand." Each thousand impressions is used to calculate the cost of CPM advertising. If the CPM rate is $10, for instance, this indicates that advertisers pay $10 for every thousand impressions of their ads.

3. Benefits and Drawbacks of CPM Advertising

The benefits of CPM advertising include: • Brand exposure and visibility: CPM advertising increases brand exposure by reaching a broad audience and creating impressions. Advertisers can present their brand to prospective customers, increasing recognition and awareness.

• Possibility of cost savings: CPM advertising is often less expensive than CPC or CPA strategies.

• Targeting capabilities: CPM advertising platforms frequently offer advanced targeting options, allowing advertisers to reach specific demographics, interests, locations, or behavior segments for a set amount of ad impressions, regardless of how many clicks or conversions they result in.

Adverse Effects of CPM Marketing

• Lack of guaranteed conversions: CPM advertising does not provide click-through or conversion guarantees like CPC or CPA models offer. Advertisers might pay for impressions that don't lead to any significant interactions or actions.

• Potential budget waste: If an advertisement fails to connect with the target market or is not well optimized, advertisers risk spending money on impressions that have no bearing on their marketing objectives.

• Less direct control over performance: Because CPM is impression-focused, advertisers have less direct control over certain processes or results. To evaluate the success of CPM campaigns, more tracking and analysis are needed.

4. Contextualizing CPM Advertising

CPM advertising's place in marketing goals:

CPM advertising is essential for reaching a number of marketing goals, such as:

• Brand awareness: CPM marketing assists companies in expanding the visibility and exposure of their brands, reaching a wider audience, and fostering familiarity with their goods or services.

• Lead generation: CPM advertising can spark interest and gather potential leads for subsequent nurturing and conversion by producing impressions and reaching a wide audience.

• consumer acquisition: CPM advertising can direct traffic to product or landing pages, which in turn facilitates consumer purchase.

Readers can get a basic understanding of CPM advertising in the context of digital marketing from the introductory chapter. Readers will be able to choose whether to use CPM in their advertising strategy with more knowledge of what it is, how it works, and its benefits and drawbacks. In the modern digital environment, understanding CPM advertising is crucial for organizations to successfully reach their target customers and meet their marketing objectives.

Chapter Two

How CPM Advertising Works

We will delve into the world of CPM advertising in this chapter and examine its fundamental ideas, methods of computation, and key performance indicators for CPM campaigns. We will obtain a thorough understanding of CPM advertising's operation and effect on the marketing industry through real-world examples.

The Foundational Elements of CPM Advertising

The term "CPM" stands for "cost per mille," where "mille" is the Latin word for "thousand" and refers to the number of impressions an ad receives. Impressions describe the frequency with which an advertisement appears on a website or application. Regardless of whether viewers click on the advertisement or take any other action, CPM advertising enables advertisers to reach a large audience and build brand awareness.

Let's assume a scenario utilizing an online shoe retailer to better understand the guiding principles of CPM advertising. The store chooses to launch a CPM advertising campaign on a well-known fashion blog. They seek to raise awareness of their most recent shoe collection and their brand. The shop will pay a predetermined CPM fee to have their advertisements shown to a specific number of blog readers, regardless of whether those readers interact with the advertising or not.

CPM Calculation and Measurement

Calculating CPM involves two essential variables: the overall number of impressions and the cost of the advertising campaign. The following equation can be used to calculate CPM:

CPM is equal to 1,000 times (Cost of the Campaign / Total Impressions).

For instance, the CPM would be computed as follows: CPM = ($2,000/500,000) x 1,000 = $4 if the online shoe company spent $2,000 on their CPM ad campaign on the fashion site.

The CPM pricing for the online shoe merchant would be $4 for every 1,000 impressions.

Advertisers frequently use impression-based metrics like the click-through rate (CTR), engagement rate, and conversion rate to assess the success of a CPM campaign. By analyzing these metrics, advertisers can gain insights into the success of their ads, understand user behavior, and optimize their future ad campaigns accordingly.

Key Metrics for Evaluating CPM Campaigns

Let's return to our example of the online shoe retailer's CPM ad campaign on the fashion blog to explore the essential metrics for evaluating its effectiveness.

1. Click-Through Rate (CTR): CTR The retailer would use the CTR to determine the level of engagement their ads received and the overall success of their campaign. The CTR measures the percentage of users who clicked on the ad after viewing it. A higher CTR indicates that the ad has captured the audience's attention and enticed them to interact further.

2. Engagement Rate: The engagement rate encompasses various user actions beyond clicks, such as social media shares, comments, or video views. Tracking the engagement rate allows the retailer to assess the ad's impact and how well it resonated with the target audience.

3. Conversion Rate: The conversion rate measures the percentage of users who not only clicked on the ad but also completed a desired action, such as making a purchase or subscribing to a newsletter. By monitoring the conversion rate, the retailer can assess the campaign's ability to generate desired outcomes and determine its return on investment.

By carefully evaluating these key metrics, advertisers can gain valuable insights into the performance of their CPM campaigns. These metrics serve as critical indicators, enabling advertisers to make informed decisions and optimize their future advertising strategies for maximum effectiveness.

We have explored the underlying principles of CPM advertising, examined the calculation and measurement methods for CPM, and identified key metrics for evaluating the success of CPM campaigns. By understanding how CPM advertising works and utilizing appropriate metrics, advertisers can optimize their campaigns to heighten brand visibility, engage their audience, and achieve desired outcomes. The real-world examples provided have showcased the practical application of CPM advertising, highlighting its potential for creating brand exposure in the ever-evolving world of digital marketing.

Chapter Three

Choosing the Right CPM Advertising Platform

The notion of CPM advertising and its significance in generating traffic and income were discussed in the previous chapter. We will now go into greater detail on how to choose the CPM advertising platform that is best for your company. We'll go through the many kinds of CPM advertising platforms, things to take into account when selecting a platform, and look at some well-known CPM advertising platforms along with their unique characteristics.

Section 1: Different Types of CPM Advertising Platforms

1. **Self-Serve CPM Advertising Platforms:** Self-serve CPM advertising platforms provide advertisers with direct control over their campaigns. These platforms allow advertisers to create, manage, and optimize their ad campaigns independently. They offer flexibility, transparency, and often have lower costs compared to managed platforms. Examples of self-serve CPM advertising platforms include Google

Ads, Facebook Ads Manager, and Amazon Advertising.

2. **Managed CPM Advertising Platforms:** Managed CPM advertising platforms offer personalized support and hands-on expertise to advertisers. These platforms assign dedicated account managers who assist in campaign setup, optimization, and provide valuable insights. Managed platforms are ideal for businesses with limited advertising resources or those seeking professional guidance. Some notable examples of managed CPM advertising platforms are The Trade Desk, MediaMath, and Amazon DSP.

3. **Programmatic CPM Advertising Platforms:** Programmatic CPM advertising platforms leverage automated technology to buy and sell ad inventory in real-time. These platforms use machine learning algorithms and artificial intelligence to optimize ad placement and targeting, resulting in more effective campaigns. The programmatic approach streamlines the advertising process, allowing advertisers to reach their target

audience efficiently. Key programmatic CPM advertising platforms include Google Marketing Platform, AdRoll, and Criteo.

Section 2: Factors to Consider When Selecting a Platform

1.   Target Audience: Take into account the precise characteristics, preferences, and behavioural patterns of your target audience. To guarantee that the correct people see your advertising at the right moment, look for a platform that has powerful targeting capabilities.

2.   Examine your spending plan and the pricing structures provided by various sites. While some platforms use performance-based pricing or dynamic bidding, others impose a set cost per thousand impressions (CPM) fee. Pick a platform that fits your aims and budget.

3.   Reporting and Analytics: To evaluate the effectiveness of your advertising efforts, you need to have access to robust reporting and analytics solutions. To properly track campaign results, look for solutions that offer detailed reporting dashboards, real-time data, conversion tracking, and other analytical tools.

4.   Ad forms and Creative Capabilities: Take into account the many ad forms that the platform supports. Make that the platform gives the flexibility to match your creative demands and maximize engagement with your audience, whether it be through display advertisements, video ads, native ads, or other forms.

Section 3: Popular CPM Advertising Platforms and Their Features

1.   One of the most popular self-serve CPM advertising platforms is Google Ads (previously Google AdWords). Numerous targeting possibilities are available, such as audience demographics, interests, and behaviors. Advertisers have a variety of ad styles to select from, including text, display, video, and others. Google Ads offers comprehensive analytics, conversion monitoring, and an easy-to-use interface for managing campaigns.

2.   The Trade Desk: A renowned managed CPM advertising platform with strong programmatic features, The Trade Desk. Advanced audience targeting, cross-device and cross-channel functionality, and access to a sizable publisher and media outlet inventory are also provided. To efficiently optimize campaigns, The Trade Desk offers

comprehensive reporting, real-time bidding, and customization possibilities.

3.   Amazon Advertising: Exclusively on the Amazon ecosystem, Amazon Advertising provides a self-serve platform for CPM advertising. Advertisers can focus their advertising to particular product categories, consumer interests, or search queries by making use of Amazon's extensive customer data. Amazon Advertising is a fantastic option for eCommerce firms thanks to its comprehensive reporting features and access to Amazon's devoted consumer base.

In order to select the best CPM advertising platform, it is important to carefully consider your company's needs, target market, spending power, and desired results. Your advertising success can be greatly impacted by choosing the right platform, whether it be a self-serve, managed, or programmatic platform, as well as taking into account elements like audience targeting, pricing models, reporting, and ad formats. You can decide how to best use your CPM advertising budget by investigating well-known sites like Google Ads, The Trade Desk, and Amazon Advertising.

Chapter Four

Creating Effective CPM Ad Campaigns

Running effective ad campaigns is crucial for businesses in the modern digital environment to reach their target audience and provide the required results. Cost Per Thousand Impressions (CPM) advertising is very common, so it's important to know how to build and optimize CPM campaigns. In this chapter, we'll examine the essential elements of creating effective CPM ad campaigns, such as establishing the campaign's objectives and goals, choosing the appropriate audience to target, creating eye-catching ad creative, and utilizing A/B testing for optimization.

Section 1: Setting Campaign Objectives and Goals

It's crucial to establish specific objectives and targets that complement your overall marketing strategy before launching a CPM ad campaign. These goals serve as indicators of campaign performance and direct decision-making throughout the campaign's lifecycle. Let's examine some instances of campaign aims and goals in the actual world:

1.   Increasing Brand Awareness

Objective: Increase brand visibility and recognition within the target market by 25%.

Goal: Achieve a 10% increase in brand-related searches and a 20% surge in social media followers.

2.   Driving Website Traffic

Objective: Generate a 50% increase in website visits from the target audience.

Goal: Achieve a 5% click-through rate (CTR) on the ad creatives and redirect visitors to relevant landing pages.

3.   Boosting Lead Generation

Objective: Collect 500 qualified leads for the sales team.

Goal: Maintain a cost per lead (CPL) below $5, and ensure a 20% conversion rate on the landing page.

Section 2: Targeting the Right Audience for Maximum Impact

Reaching the right audience is crucial to maximize the impact of your CPM ad campaign. Identifying your target audience helps optimize ad spend and ensures that your message resonates with those most likely to convert. Consider the following examples of effective audience targeting:

1. Demographic Targeting

Target audience: Women aged 25-34 who reside in urban areas and have an interest in fitness and wellness.

2. Behavioral Targeting

Target audience: Users who have recently searched for "best budget smartphones" or "affordable phone plans."

3. Retargeting

Target audience: Users who previously visited your website and added items to their cart but did not complete the purchase.

Section 3: Designing Compelling Ad Creatives

Ad creatives play a vital role in capturing audience attention and effectively conveying your brand message. Here are some real-world examples of compelling ad creative across various platforms:

1.   Display Ads: An e-commerce company showcases a visually appealing product image along with a limited-time offer, leveraging persuasive copy and a clear call-to-action.

2.   Video Ads: A fitness equipment brand demonstrates the versatility and ease of use of their product through a captivating video, emphasizing real people achieving fitness goals.

3.   Native Ads: A travel agency integrates their promotional content seamlessly within a popular travel guide website, offering valuable tips and promoting personalized travel itineraries.

Section 4: A/B Testing and Optimizing CPM Campaigns

Once your CPM ad campaign is live, it's essential to continually optimize and improve its performance. A/B testing allows you to experiment with different variables to identify the most effective strategies. Here are a few examples of A/B testing scenarios:

1.   Testing Ad Formats: Compare the performance of display ads and video ads to determine which format generates higher engagement and conversions.

2.   Testing Call-to-Action Buttons: Evaluate whether using phrases like "Shop Now" or "Learn More" in your CTA buttons influences click-through rates and conversion rates.

3.   Testing Ad Placements: Analyze the performance of ad placements on different platforms or websites to identify the highest performing placements for your target audience.

Creating effective CPM ad campaigns requires careful planning, precise audience targeting, compelling ad creatives, and continual optimization through A/B testing. By setting clear campaign objectives, defining target audiences, crafting engaging ad creatives, and refining campaigns through testing, businesses can position themselves for success in the competitive digital advertising landscape.

Chapter Five

CPM Advertising Strategies

Online advertising is now a crucial component of marketing plans for companies across all industries in the digital age. Advertising with a cost per thousand impressions (CPM) model is one such tactic that enables companies to successfully reach their target market. The several CPM advertising tactics will be covered in this chapter, including brand awareness campaigns, direct response campaigns, retargeting strategies, and mobile and video ad strategies. We will show how these tactics can be used to maximize the return on investment through specific, real-world scenarios.

Section 1: Brand Awareness Campaigns

Brand recognition is essential for any company to stand out from rivals and develop a devoted clientele. CPM advertising has the potential to significantly improve brand recognition and visibility. Let's use the debut of an organic product line by a skincare company as an example. They choose to launch a CPM ad campaign across well-known lifestyle websites in order to increase brand awareness.

By focusing on customers who are interested in skincare, cosmetics, and natural products, the brand makes sure that their advertisement is prominently presented to the target market. The amount of impressions and click-through rates a campaign receives can be used to gauge its effectiveness. These indicators will show how far and how well the brand's message is being received, which will ultimately increase its market presence.

Section 2: Direct Response Campaigns

The goal of direct response marketing is to get the target audience to take instant action, like buying something or subscribing to a newsletter. CPM marketing has the potential to be a potent instrument for evoking such reactions. Let's look at an e-commerce firm conducting a 24-hour flash sale as an example.

The brand begins a CPM ad campaign aimed at their existing customer base and new customers with interests compatible with their offerings in order to create urgency and boost conversions. Users are sent to a special landing page where they may make a purchase by the advertisement, which clearly displays the limited-time deal. The brand may assess the success of their direct response campaign and make any adjustments to their plan by keeping an eye on the click-through rate and conversion rate.

Section 3: Retargeting Strategies using CPM Advertising

Retargeting is a common tactic used to interact with consumers who have previously expressed interest in a brand's goods or services. By ensuring that the brand's message remains top-of-mind for potential customers, CPM advertising can be an effective strategy in retargeting efforts. Let's use an online clothes business as an example. The retailer wishes to re-engage customers who have abandoned their shopping carts.

By adding things to their carts but abandoning the checkout process, consumers have shown their intent to make a purchase, and the brand can target them with targeted adverts using CPM advertising. These advertisements may feature the abandoned goods, luring customers back to finish their purchase. The brand may improve their retargeting approach and increase sales by regularly analyzing the click-through rate, conversion rate, and cart abandonment rate.

Section 4: Mobile and Video Ad Strategies

As mobile usage continues to rise, leveraging Mobile and video CPM advertising can offer a variety of lucrative business alternatives. Let's use the launch of a new feature by a meal delivery app that targets professionals with busy schedules as an example.

The app may draw in their target audience's attention by displaying interesting video adverts on well-known productivity and lifestyle apps utilizing CPM advertising. These video advertisements can persuade viewers to download and utilize the app by highlighting its user-friendly interface, time-saving features, and mouthwatering meal alternatives. Metrics like the rate of completed videos, app downloads, and average order value can be used to gauge success.

CPM advertising tactics give organizations a variety of options for achieving their marketing objectives. In today's cutthroat digital environment, CPM advertising can be an effective tool for generating fast replies, building brand awareness, retargeting potential consumers, or engaging mobile and video viewers. Businesses can boost their visibility, conversions, and overall market performance by properly planning and managing these methods.

Chapter Six

Budgeting and Pricing Models in CPM Advertising

We will go into the specifics of CPM (Cost Per Thousand Impressions) advertising budgeting and pricing models in this chapter. We will look at how CPM bid prices are established, how budgets for CPM campaigns are allocated, and methods for maximizing ROI (Return on Investment) in CPM advertising. You will have a thorough understanding of how to successfully manage your resources to drive successful CPM advertising campaigns by the end of this chapter.

1.   Determining CPM Bid Prices:

One of the primary challenges in CPM advertising is determining the appropriate bid prices that provide value for your campaign. To do this, you need to analyze various factors, including target audience, campaign objectives, and competitor analysis.

Real-world Example

Imagine you are a fashion retailer looking to promote your new summer collection through CPM advertising. You conduct market research and identify your target audience: young women aged 18-30 who love street fashion. Based on this information, you evaluate the pricing strategies employed by competing fashion brands targeting a similar audience. You find that their CPM bid prices fall between $4 and $6. Taking into account your campaign goals and budget, you decide to set your CPM bid price at $5. This price strikes a balance between affordability and effectively reaching your target audience.

2   Understanding Budget Allocation for CPM Campaigns:

Once you have determined your CPM bid prices, it is crucial to allocate your budget effectively across different channels and campaigns. Proper budget allocation ensures that you maximize the impact of your advertising efforts within your financial constraints.

Real-world Example

Continuing with our fashion retailer example, you have set a budget of $10,000 for your CPM campaign. Considering that your target audience includes young women, you decide to allocate a significant portion of your budget toward popular social media platforms, such as Instagram and Facebook, as they have a higher concentration of your target demographic. You allocate $6,000 for social media advertising, $2,000 for influencer collaborations, $1,500 for display advertising on fashion websites, and $500 for retargeting ads. This budget allocation strategy enables you to diversify your reach while focusing on channels that are likely to yield the highest returns.

3.   Strategies for Maximizing ROI in CPM Advertising:

To truly make the most of your CPM advertising budget, it is essential to adopt strategies that optimize return on investment. This involves continuous monitoring and optimization of your campaigns, utilizing advanced targeting techniques, and leveraging data analytics for insights.

Real-world Example

Returning to our fashion retailer, you closely monitor the performance of your CPM campaigns across different channels. After a couple of weeks, you notice that social media platforms are driving the highest click-through rates and conversions, generating the highest ROI. You decide to reallocate a portion of your budget away from less effective channels, such as display advertising on fashion websites, and invest more in social media advertising. Additionally, you leverage data analytics to identify the best-performing age groups and locations within your target audience, enabling you to refine your targeting further. These strategic adjustments allow you to maximize your ROI by focusing your resources on the most promising opportunities.

Budgeting and pricing models play a pivotal role in successful CPM advertising campaigns. Determining CPM bid prices, understanding budget allocation, and implementing strategies for maximizing ROI are essential components of any comprehensive advertising strategy. By employing these techniques and continuously evaluating your campaigns, you can optimize your budget utilization and achieve the desired results in CPM advertising.

Chapter Seven

Monitoring and Analyzing CPM Ad Performance

This chapter will go in-depth on the value of tracking and evaluating CPM (Cost Per Thousand Impressions) ad campaign performance. We will investigate the methods for monitoring and evaluating campaign performance, deciphering key performance indicators (KPIs), and applying tools and methods for CPM ad data analysis. You will learn useful tips for efficiently monitoring and optimizing your CPM ad campaigns with an emphasis on real-world examples.

1. Tracking and Measuring CPM Campaign Performance:

Tracking and measuring the performance of CPM campaigns is essential for understanding their effectiveness and identifying areas for improvement. Setting up proper tracking mechanisms and utilizing analytics tools allow you to evaluate various metrics and make data-driven decisions.

Real-world Example

Consider a software company running a CPM campaign to promote their new project management tool. They set up tracking pixels on their website and landing pages to monitor user interactions. By using tools like Google Analytics or a dedicated ad tracking platform, they can measure metrics such as impressions, clicks, click-through rate (CTR), conversions, bounce rate, and average session duration. Through this tracking, they can assess how well their campaign is driving engagement and conversions, enabling them to optimize their strategies accordingly.

2. Interpreting Key Performance Indicators (KPIs)

Key performance indicators (KPIs) provide insights into the effectiveness of CPM campaigns. Analyzing and interpreting these indicators helps you understand which aspects of your campaign are performing well and where there may be room for improvement.

Real-world Example

Suppose an e-commerce retailer is running a CPM campaign to promote their summer clothing collection. They analyze various KPIs, including CTR, conversion rate, cost-per-conversion, and return on ad spend (ROAS). They find that their CTR is moderately high, indicating a strong initial engagement.

However, their conversion rate is relatively low, suggesting a need to enhance the effectiveness of their landing page or optimize their targeting. By closely monitoring these KPIs, they can identify the bottlenecks in their campaign and take targeted actions to improve its overall performance.

3.   Tools and Techniques for Analyzing CPM Ad Data:

Various tools and techniques are available to analyze CPM ad data, providing valuable insights for optimizing campaign performance. These tools help in identifying trends, audience behavior, and areas of opportunity for improving ad targeting and messaging.

Real-world Example

Continuing with the e-commerce retailer example, they decide to use advanced analytics tools to gain deeper insights into their CPM ad data. They employ tools like Google Analytics, Facebook Ads Manager, and data visualization platforms to segment their audience by demographics, interests, and devices. By analyzing conversion paths, they discover that users who engage with their ads on mobile devices have a higher likelihood of completing a purchase. Armed with this knowledge, they optimize their campaigns to further target mobile users and allocate their budget accordingly, resulting in a more efficient use of their resources and increased conversions.

Monitoring and analyzing the performance of CPM ad campaigns is vital for optimizing their effectiveness. By tracking and measuring campaign performance, interpreting key performance indicators, and utilizing tools and techniques for data analysis, you can gain actionable insights to enhance your targeting strategies, optimize ad messaging, and drive better campaign results. With continuous monitoring and evaluation, you can iteratively improve your CPM ad campaigns and achieve your advertising goals.

Chapter Eight

Managing Ad Fraud and Click Fraud in CPM Advertising

When executing CPM (Cost Per Thousand Impressions) advertising campaigns, advertisers encounter major problems from ad fraud and click fraud. The principles of ad fraud and click fraud, their effects on campaign effectiveness, and methods for avoiding and spotting these fraudulent practices will all be covered in this chapter. To assist you comprehend the practical ramifications of handling ad fraud and click fraud in CPM advertising, we will give you in-depth examples from the real world.

1. Understanding Ad Fraud and Click Fraud:

Any fraudulent conduct intended to fool advertisers and falsely depict the efficacy and value of their advertising campaigns is referred to as "ad fraud." In order to artificially boost click-through rates (CTR) and deplete advertising expenditures, click fraud, in particular, entails the creation of phony clicks on ads. Ad fraud and click fraud have a negative influence on campaign success because they waste ad spend, skew performance indicators, and lower ROI.

Real-world Example

Consider an online retailer that launches a CPM advertising campaign to highlight a new product range. They observe that there are disproportionately more clicks on their campaign than there are conversions. After further inquiry, they learn that a sizable fraction of these clicks originate from dubious sources, including click farms or bots. This suggests that click fraud is present, in which false clicks are produced to use up their advertising budget without providing any genuine value in terms of client engagement or conversions.

2. Common Types of Ad Fraud and Their Impact

Advertisers should be aware of the various prevalent types of ad fraud because each one affects the effectiveness of campaigns in a different way. The most common types of ad fraud include ad stacking, bot traffic, domain spoofing, and impression fraud. These dishonest practices may lead to wasted advertising dollars, distorted performance indicators, and diminished campaign efficacy.

Real-world Example

Take the example of a mobile app developer who launches a CPM advertising campaign to attract new users to their gaming game. They find that a considerable portion of impressions come from questionable sources, inflating impression metrics. Further research reveals that these impressions are produced by fake bots rather than actual users. As a result, their advertising spend is squandered on non-human traffic that does not help them find actual app users, which compromises the effectiveness of their campaign.

3. Prevention and Detection Strategies for Ad Fraud

Preventing and detecting ad fraud is crucial for maintaining the integrity of CPM advertising campaigns. Implementing robust prevention and detection strategies helps advertisers minimize the impact of fraudulent activities and protect their ad budgets. Some effective strategies include using ad verification services, implementing fraud protection tools, monitoring traffic patterns, and utilizing real-time analytics.

Real-world Example

Using the mobile app developer as an example, they decide to put in place a thorough ad fraud prevention plan. They collaborate with an ad verification service that employs sophisticated algorithms to recognize and weed out phony impressions and clicks. Additionally, they use fraud prevention tools to track traffic patterns and spot shady activity, like high click-through rates from particular IP addresses or click farms. In order to identify traffic anomalies and flag potential cases of ad fraud, they also use real-time analytics. By implementing these prevention and detection strategies, the app developer significantly reduces the impact of ad fraud on their campaign performance and preserves their ad budget for genuine user acquisition.

Managing ad fraud and click fraud is paramount for advertisers running CPM advertising campaigns. By understanding the various types of ad fraud, their impact on campaign performance, and implementing prevention and detection strategies, advertisers can mitigate the risks and protect their ad budgets. Real-world examples highlight the practical implications of managing ad fraud and underline the importance of investing in proactive measures to ensure the effectiveness and integrity of CPM advertising campaigns.

Chapter Nine

Future Trends in CPM Advertising

CPM (Cost Per Thousand Impressions) advertising is an evolving field that constantly adapts to new technologies, consumer behaviors, and market trends. In this chapter, we will explore the future trends in CPM advertising and their potential impact on campaign strategies. We will discuss emerging technologies, new formats and channels, as well as provide predictions for the future of CPM advertising, supported by detailed real-world examples.

1. Emerging technologies and their impact on CPM advertising

Advancements in technology have a significant impact on the effectiveness and efficiency of CPM advertising campaigns. New technologies, such as artificial intelligence (AI), augmented reality (AR), and machine learning (ML), are revolutionizing the way advertisers target, engage, and convert consumers. These technologies enable personalized advertising experiences, real-time optimization, and improved ad targeting, ultimately enhancing the ROI for advertisers.

Real-world Example

Consider a travel agency running a CPM ad campaign to promote their vacation packages. They leverage AI-powered recommendation engines to deliver personalized ads to potential customers. The recommendation engine analyzes user behavior, preferences, and previous interactions to present highly relevant and targeted ad content. This personalized approach increases the likelihood of engagement and conversions, resulting in a higher ROI for the travel agency.

2.   New formats and channels in CPM advertising

As consumer behaviors shift and new platforms emerge, advertisers must adapt their CPM advertising strategies to reach their target audience effectively. New formats, such as video ads, interactive ads, and native ads, provide opportunities for enhanced engagement and increased brand awareness. Additionally, emerging channels, including social media platforms, streaming services, and voice-activated devices, offer new avenues for advertisers to reach and connect with their target audience.

Real-world Example

Suppose a beverage company wants to launch a new energy drink and reach a younger demographic. They decide to incorporate video ads into their CPM advertising campaign and distribute them through popular social media platforms, such as Instagram and TikTok. By leveraging the rapid growth and engagement of video content on these platforms, the beverage company effectively engages with their target audience, creating viral campaigns that lead to increased brand awareness and product sales.

3.   Predictions for the future of CPM advertising:

The future of CPM advertising is dynamic and constantly evolving. As technology continues to advance and consumer behaviors change, several predictions can be made for the future of CPM advertising. These predictions include increased personalization through data-driven insights, the rise of programmatic advertising, integration with smart devices and the Internet of Things (IoT), and the growth of immersive ad experiences through virtual and augmented reality.

Real-world Example

Imagine a retail brand that wants to maximize their ad campaign's impact by leveraging emerging technologies. They partner with an advertising agency that specializes in programmatic advertising and leverages data-driven insights to optimize ad placements in real-time. By integrating their CPM advertising campaigns with various smart devices, such as smart TVs and voice-activated speakers, they ensure seamless brand exposure throughout a consumer's day. Additionally, they invest in immersive ad experiences, creating interactive virtual reality demonstrations of their products. These immersive experiences not only engage customers but also provide valuable data and insights that enhance future campaign strategies.

The future of CPM advertising is exciting and full of opportunities for advertisers. With the rapid advancements in technology, emerging formats and channels, and predictions for the future, advertisers must stay ahead of the curve to remain competitive. Real-world examples illustrate the practical implications and successes of embracing emerging technologies and trends in CPM advertising. By adapting to the future trends in CPM advertising, advertisers can effectively engage their target audience, optimize campaign performance, and achieve their marketing objectives.

Chapter Ten

Case Studies and Success Stories in CPM Advertising

This chapter will explore successful case studies and real-world examples of how CPM (Cost Per Thousand Impressions) advertising strategies have impacted various industries. These examples, which highlight the plans, tactics, and results of top CPM advertisers, will offer insightful information and lessons gained. Advertisers can find ideas and advice for their own CPM advertising campaigns by studying these case studies.

1. Nike's "Dream Crazier" Video Campaign

Nike, a renowned sportswear brand, launched a CPM advertising campaign titled "Dream Crazier" centered around empowering women in sports. They utilized video ads to create an emotional narrative that resonated with their target audience. By leveraging platforms such as YouTube and social media, Nike was able to reach millions of viewers.

Insights and Lessons Learned:

- Emotional storytelling can create a strong connection with the audience, enhancing engagement and brand loyalty.

- Utilizing video ads allows for a visually compelling and immersive experience, increasing the impact of the message.

- Leveraging popular platforms and social media channels maximizes reach and engagement.

2. Coca-Cola's Personalized Holiday Campaign:

Coca-Cola implemented a CPM advertising campaign during the holiday season that featured personalized ads. They used data-driven insights to create tailored ads that addressed individuals by name and incorporated their location. This personalized approach increased customer engagement and brand loyalty.

Insights and Lessons Learned:

- Personalization can significantly enhance the effectiveness of CPM advertising, creating a deeper connection with the audience.

- Utilizing data-driven insights enables advertisers to deliver highly relevant and targeted ads, resulting in increased engagement and conversions.

- Holidays and special occasions provide opportunities to create memorable and shareable ad experiences.

3. Airbnb's Dynamic Retargeting Campaign

Airbnb, a popular online marketplace for lodging rentals, implemented a dynamic retargeting campaign using CPM advertising. They displayed personalized ads to users who had previously visited their website and viewed specific properties. These ads showcased relevant accommodations, enticing users to complete their bookings.

Insights and Lessons Learned:

- Retargeting campaigns can effectively re-engage potential customers by displaying personalized and relevant ads.

- Dynamic retargeting allows for real-time ad optimization, ensuring advertisements are continuously updated with the most current and relevant inventory.

- Utilizing CPM advertising for retargeting efforts helps improve conversion rates and maximizes the ROI of advertising spend.

## 4.	Amazon's Voice-Activated Advertising:

Amazon, the e-commerce giant, introduced voice-activated advertising through their Alexa-enabled devices. Advertisers can leverage CPM advertising to reach users through audio ads delivered via these smart speakers. Companies such as Procter & Gamble and Purina have successfully embraced this new advertising channel to expand their reach and engage with their target audience.

Insights and Lessons Learned:

- Integrating CPM advertising with voice-activated devices provides new opportunities to connect with consumers in their everyday lives.

- Voice-activated ads can be personalized and contextually relevant, creating a seamless and immersive brand experience.

- Early adoption of new channels can provide a competitive advantage and help establish brand presence in emerging markets.

The case studies and success stories discussed in this chapter offer valuable insights and lessons learned from top CPM advertisers. These real-world examples highlight the importance of emotional storytelling, personalized advertising, dynamic retargeting, and embracing emerging channels. Advertisers can leverage these insights to inform their own CPM advertising strategies and maximize the effectiveness and impact of their campaigns. By analyzing and learning from these successful campaigns, advertisers can optimize their targeting, engagement, and conversion strategies, ultimately achieving their marketing objectives.

Chapter Eleven

Conclusion and Next Steps

As we come to the end of this book, it's important to recap the key takeaways from the previous chapters and provide actionable tips and recommendations for implementing CPM (Cost Per Thousand Impressions) advertising strategies. Additionally, we will provide resources for further learning and exploration to help advertisers stay updated on the latest trends and best practices in CPM advertising.

Recap of Key Takeaways:

1. Understanding CPM Advertising: CPM advertising is a pricing model where advertisers pay for every thousand impressions of their ad. It is essential to have a clear understanding of CPM and its advantages, such as greater control over advertising costs and increased brand visibility.

2. Targeting and Segmentation: Effective targeting and segmentation strategies are crucial for CPM advertising success. By identifying and understanding the characteristics and needs of your target audience, you can develop personalized

and relevant ads that maximize engagement and conversions.

3. Creative and Compelling Ad Content: Creating creative and compelling ad content is essential to capturing audience attention and driving engagement. Utilize visually appealing images, captivating headlines, and persuasive call-to-actions to maximize click-through rates and conversions.

4. Tracking and Analytics: Utilize tracking and analytics tools to measure the performance of your CPM advertising campaigns. Monitoring key metrics such as impressions, click-through rates, conversions, and cost per conversion can provide valuable insights and help optimize future campaigns.

5. Testing and Optimization: A continuous testing and optimization approach is necessary to maximize the effectiveness of CPM advertising campaigns. Experiment with different ad formats, targeting options, and messaging to identify what works best for your audience and goals.

Actionable Tips and Recommendations:

1. Set Clear Objectives: Start by setting clear objectives for your CPM advertising campaigns. Whether it's increasing brand awareness, driving website traffic, or generating conversions, having defined goals will guide your strategies and help measure success.

2. Establish Key Performance Indicators (KPIs): Determine the metrics that align with your objectives and establish KPIs to track progress. This will provide a framework for evaluating the success of your campaigns and making data-driven optimizations.

3. Utilize Audience Insights: Take advantage of audience insights and data to improve targeting and segmentation. Dig into demographic, behavioral, and psychographic information to understand your audience's preferences, interests, and needs, which will inform your ad strategies.

4. Experiment with Different Ad Formats: CPM advertising offers various ad formats, including display ads, video ads, native ads, and social media ads.

Experimenting with different formats can help determine which ones resonate best with your target audience and yield the highest response rates.

5.   Monitor Competitor Strategies: Keep an eye on your competitors' strategies and techniques. Analyzing their successful campaigns can provide inspiration and insights for your own advertising efforts.

Resources for Further Learning and Exploration:

1.   Industry Blogs and Websites: Stay updated with the latest trends and insights in CPM advertising through industry-focused blogs and websites such as Adweek, Marketing Land, and Search Engine Journal.

2.   Online Courses and Certifications: Take advantage of online courses and certifications offered by platforms such as Google Ads, Facebook Blueprint, and HubSpot Academy. These resources provide comprehensive training on CPM advertising and related topics.

3.   Webinars and Events: Attend webinars and industry events to learn from industry experts and stay updated on

emerging trends in CPM advertising. Resources like Webinerds and Eventbrite offer a wide range of webinars and events to choose from.

4.   Networking and Peer Groups: Connect with other CPM advertisers and digital marketing professionals through networking events, LinkedIn groups, and online forums. Engaging in conversations and sharing experiences can provide valuable insights and foster professional growth.

CPM advertising offers immense opportunities for advertisers to reach, engage, and convert their target audience. By understanding the key takeaways from this book, implementing actionable tips and recommendations, and leveraging resources for further learning and exploration, advertisers can develop effective CPM advertising strategies that yield measurable results. Stay informed, adapt to industry changes, and continuously optimize your campaigns to maximize the impact and ROI of your CPM advertising efforts.

www.ingramcontent.com/pod-product-compliance
Lightning Source LLC
Chambersburg PA
CBHW071108260726
48661CB00006B/2532